Petite
PLATES

THERESA HILL

AuthorHouse™
1663 Liberty Drive
Bloomington, IN 47403
www.authorhouse.com
Phone: 1 (800) 839-8640

Published by AuthorHouse 07/21/2016

ISBN: 978-1-5246-1525-3 (sc)
ISBN: 978-1-5246-1526-0 (e)

Library of Congress Control Number: 2016910175

Print information available on the last page.

Any people depicted in stock imagery provided by Thinkstock are models, and such images are being used for illustrative purposes only. Certain stock imagery © Thinkstock.

This book is printed on acid-free paper.

The concept behind *"Petite Plates"* is portion control. I believe the supersized, overindulgent mentality many American's live by is destructive. It is evident by the statistics of our overweight society that we are what we eat and supersized says it all. My passion and menu planning is about balance. Healthy eating combined with traditional incorporating all things in moderation. The goal is to eat less, downsize and re-direct the focus to *"eat to live:* instead of *"live to eat".* I believe this begins with eating smaller portions on smaller plates. Enjoy, savor, slow down and appreciate the quality not quantity.

I was raised with the Mediterranean style of eating. Delicious food in large quantities all the time and never leave the table without cleaning the plate. I believe that leads to problems and creates poor habits later in life. As far back as I can remember I have always been an advocate for healthy eating, living and thinking. Over the years, I have enjoyed the journey of research and learning of the various ways to incorporate health into my daily lifestyle. I have observed the tragedy and triumph of people's lives being change drastically simply by what they choose to eat or not eat. It has left a strong enough impact on me that I try to carefully consider my personal choices daily as a result. People have a relationship with food and it can be a healthy one with proper perspective or an unhealthy one ruled by addictions.

I believe it is important to replenish and give back to the earth what we've taken. I love supporting farmer's markets and buying locally. The products purchased are more reliable than those from large corporations. I believe that people who are like-minded in this particular area are willing to invest their time and money for quality and those that do not, have the option to eat elsewhere.

Creating new habits are the foundation for making change; Repetition + Reward = Habit. This can be positive or negative, depending on what we purpose ourselves to strive towards. Small changes over a consistent period of time are the most lasting. Habits must be forced at first but become natural with consistency. This book will hopefully encourage, inspire and provide tips on how to begin the process so that it evolves into a lifestyle. Change is in the struggle but the benefits out way sacrifice. The world's way: cheap, fast and easy. God's way: hard, costly and time consuming but the results are enduring! A willing spirit is a teachable spirit; if you find you are challenged by being willing to make changes, I would encourage you to pray and ask God to make you willing. I have had to do that quite often over the years with regard to many areas I was resisting. I assure you that if you ask Him, He will provide you with this trait. It is required for almost any and all areas of growth and development.

Lastly, accountability and responsibility are essential to maintaining the change once the new habit has been formed. We are responsible for our own health and wellness. We should not hand that over to restaurants and processed foods and expect to feel well and be productive. If food addictions or eating disorders are an area of captivity, then we most definitely need an accountability partner to come along side to keep us honest. This will be difficult without willingness. People typically do not enjoy having their choices questioned or being called out when those choices aren't in the best interest. However, it is imperative that we assume the responsibility of our health and partner with those that are like-minded in this area. *Ecc. 4:12 "Though one may be overpowered, two can defend themselves, a cord of three strands is not quickly broken."*

I pray that this book will be a light to your path and guide to direct you when you feel lost, desperate or confused.

The Mind

I believe this is where it all begins. The mind contains our thoughts, which controls every aspect of our being. Our thoughts dictate our words, feelings and actions. The body does what the mind tells it to, so let's start feeding our mind first. I use scripture to renew and reprogram my thought life. I read them daily, almost always out loud. Joyce Meyer has said repeatedly *"We believe what we hear ourselves say more than what we hear others say"*, and speaking positively out loud builds confidence and counters the attacks of the enemy. We must speak those things that are not, as though they are; this provokes the body to respond accordingly. Ezekiel 37:4 *"Then He said to me, "Prophesy to these bones and say to them, 'dry bones, hear the Word of the Lord!'"*

You must know what you're fighting against to know what to fight with!! 1 Cor. 10:23 *"All things are permissible, but not all things are beneficial. All things are permissible, but I will not be a slave to any of them."*

Educating ourselves with regard to positive, uplifting mind-sets as well as nutrition and wellness is what will be a lasting result. I desire to teach others how and provide them with enough resources to get in the driver's seat. I don't want to do it for you and I can't. Good health is individualized and personalized; what works for one, may not work for another. Each person has their own struggles, weaknesses and lifestyles that they must work within and around. Diets, trends or supplements don't work long-term and make matters worse. They are all short-cuts, which as the word implies – short-lived, short-term. My desire is that a new lifestyle and mind-set will be formed and continuous.

One of the best ways to start changing what you eat is to use alternative ingredients that are high in nutrient density. This is also a great way to get children, especially those who are picky, to eat healthier.

Sweets!

This is an area where we really need to concentrate on reducing significantly our intake. It is my professional opinion, that sweets are more detrimental to our bodies than fat. It's not just in pure sugar form but in the foods that process or digest in the body as sugar or simple carbs. I am realistic in knowing that very few people will completely eliminate sugar, in any form, from their diets so I would encourage people to use alternative sweeteners; at least those that have nutrient value and use them in smaller quantities. Agave nectar, pure, local-grown or harvested maple sugar and honey are the ones that I use regularly. Coconut sugar is another great alternative to cane sugar. Remember that our bodies crave what we've trained them to crave through eating repetitively and consistently. If one craves sugar/sweets/processed or carb-based, then consider experimenting with fruits, yogurt parfaits or at the very least, making your own sweet treats from scratch substituting higher quality and nutrient dense items such as chia seeds, hemp seeds, Gluten-free flour blends. Remember that sweets should be enjoyed NOT in moderation but rather very sparingly; few and far, far between and when consumed, in very small amounts and if possible pair with fiber to lessen sugar spikes and help with balancing insulin levels.

Dedication

I am dedicating this book to my husband Rick. He is the stable, strong and solid foundation I lean into. I am so thankful to have him in my life. He had confidence in me when I had none; he believed in me when I doubted everything. He was certain that I could do it when I was insecure and wishy-washy. The examples he has set for me and the light of Christ he has shown me have by far, been the most loving things he has done. He is a great leader, who doesn't back down from his convictions and I have so much respect for him. He has a quiet, gentle strength that's enticing. His ability to go about his life with what seems like no fear, is a great witness for me, who struggles with just about every fear there is; he is my daily reminder that Christ died for us to live in freedom. ***Galatians 5:1*** *"It is for freedom that Christ has set us free. Stand firm, then, and do not let yourselves be burdened again by a yoke of slavery."* He is definitely the risk taker in our relationship. He's always willing to take a chance on me or on anyone whom he loves and believes in and he goes forth with the attitude, "it'll all work out, God has our backs". He trusts God and knowing that, helps me step out and want to do the same. He believes there is a reason, which is determined by God, that things either happen or don't. Sometimes we're supposed to know and sometimes we're not; having peace in those *circumstances* comes very easy to him and I need that witness in my life. ***Psalm 55:22*** *"Cast your cares on the LORD and he will sustain you; he will never let the righteous be shaken."* He has a gentle way of pulling me back from the "ledges" I get myself on emotionally. Words can't express how much I love and appreciate him; without his support and my faith and relationship with Jesus, I wouldn't have the courage to write books, start a business or go back to school. Thank you to you both!

Table of Contents

Mini-Sides:

Mini-Mains Dishes

Mini-Sweet Endings

MINI-BEGINNINGS:
(Breakfast, Appetizers, Soups, Salads, Dips)

Artichoke and Asparagus Panzanella

4-5 slices of day-old bread, cubed
1 c black pitted olives, drained/rinsed
2 cloves garlic, minced
8- grape tomatoes, halved
1 bunch fresh asparagus, cut into thirds

6 Spanish, green olives, drained/rinsed
8-oz of frozen/thawed artichokes or canned, drained
Pecorino or Parmesan to top

Vinaigrette ingredients: 1 lemon zested and juiced, tsp. Dijon mustard, 1 c fresh parsley, tsp. dried basil, salt, pepper, ¼ c olive or grapeseed oil and 2 Tbsp. cider vinegar. *(can be made in blender or whisked together in a bowl)*

I love to use leftover, homemade bread for this dish but any type will work; toasted Ezekiel bread works great!

Preheat oven to 425. On a silicone or parchment line baking sheet, place artichokes, asparagus and minced garlic on sheet; drizzle with olive oil, salt and pepper and roast for 20 minutes or until tender but still firm. Remove and allow to cool. In large serving bowl, place cubed bread and all remaining ingredients. Top with the Vinaigrette and toss well to combine. Before serving add the shaved or grated cheese, if using.

Cooked, cooled cubed chicken can be added to this to make a main meal and increase protein.

Artichoke and Olive Tapenade

9 oz. box frozen artichokes, thawed, chopped
1 whole tomato, chopped
½ tsp. each dried parsley, basil, oregano
half of lemon or lime, zested & juiced
¼ c green olives, drained

¼ c green and black olives
Tbsp. minced chives, optional
pinch salt, pepper
olive oil

Place all ingredients in bowl and toss well to combine. Cover and refrigerate for 30 minutes to marry flavors. Taste and readjust if needed.

Serving options:
- ☞ Serve on grilled piece of gluten-free bread
- ☞ Serve on top of freshly grilled or baked tilapia or any fish
- ☞ Serve on top of dark greens or in a lettuce cup
- ☞ Served in endive leaves! My favorite!
- ☞ Serve with whole-grain chips, crackers or fresh cut vegetables

From my Flatbread Focaccia recipe in this book, there are 3-other options for using up the dough from 1-recipe. So it's an economical and effective option. This is the first of many:

Avocado Cream and Flatbread Salad

1-flatbread, grilled and cooled
Mixed greens (spinach, arugula, collard)

Goat Cheese, to crumble on top
Tomatoes, sliced

Avocado Cream: 1 avocado, peeled and seed removed, ½ lemon zested & juiced, ½ c Greek plain yogurt, salt, pepper, 1-c fresh parsley

In food processor, make the avocado cream until smooth consistency. Spread over cooled flatbread, top with any type or various types of dark leafy greens, slices of tomato and top with crumbled goat cheese (or Feta can be substituted).

Cooked, cooled chicken or turkey may be added, as well as white beans.

Warm Black Rice & Lentil Salad

1 garlic clove, minced

1 c black rice, cooked

1 c fresh parsley, minced

1 c sugar snap peas, chopped

1 celery stalk, chopped

1 c cherry tomatoes, halved

½ c carrot, minced

1 c sprouted lentil trio, cooked

1 c fresh broccoli flowerets, chopped

½ c chicken broth

½ sm. Onion, minced

Vinaigrette: tsp. ground coriander, salt, pepper, ½ tsp. cumin, 1 ¼ tsp. dried basil & oregano, ¼ tsp. chili powder, ¼ c feta cheese crumbles, zest & juice of 1-lemon, 1-Tbsp. vinegar, 1-tsp. honey, ½ c oil

Sauté the minced garlic, onion and carrot in 2-Tbsp olive oil and ½ c chicken broth over medium heat until soft, tender and moisture evaporates. Add cooked rice, lentils, all vegetables to a large mixing bowl. Add the cooked garlic, onion, vinaigrette, minced parsley and stir well to coat and combine.

Notes:

➢ Any vegetables can be used

➢ Great as a filler for collard leaf, quesadilla or pita wraps

➢ Best served warm, but can be served cold or room temp

Blueberry Vinaigrette
(makes about 1-quart jar)

2 c Blueberries (fresh)
1 Tbsp. red wine vinegar
2 Tbsp. Greek yogurt – plain
3 sprig mint
Pinch of dry oregano
¼ - ½ c canola oil

Zest & Juice of 2-limes & 1 lemon
2 Tbsp. honey
2 chive sprigs - fresh
2 spring basil & parsley - fresh
salt & pepper to taste
¼ c water

Use blender to combine all ingredients thoroughly. Refrigerate for up to 3-days.

The benefits of homemade bone broth are unbelievable; it contains collagen, minerals, vitamins, anti-oxidants; the list goes on. I would encourage you to check online for additional information. Its uses are varied as well; soups, stews, sauces, or sip it hot. It's great for using up leftover veggies and economizes the purchasing of whole poultry.

Bone Broth!

2 Carrot
3" piece ginger root
5-8 Bella mushrooms
3 celery stalk

2 small tomatoes
3 garlic cloves
1 onion
Carcass of cooked & cooled chicken or turkey

Spices: 2-bay leaves, 2-sprigs rosemary, 3-sprigs thyme, zest and juice of 1-lemon, 2-tbsp tomato paste, salt/pepper, tsp. dried oregano, basil, and fennel seed

- 👍 Fresh fennel bulb can also be added
- 👍 5 Radish can also be added
- 👍 Dried herbs can be used in place of fresh (start with tsp of each)
- 👍 Can be made spicy by adding cayenne
- 👍 Veggies can be halved, garlic left whole. Due to the long cooking time, size is irrelevant as they are going to break completely down and be discarded at the end

Cook, cool and remove all flesh from a whole chicken or turkey. Place carcass into a large stock pot. Add all veggies and spices. Cover with cold water and 2-cup ice. Be sure the bones/veggies are completely submerged. Bring to boil, reduce heat to low and simmer for a minimum of 12 hours and up to 24.

Strain out all items with a large sieve – discard. Let the broth cool completely before refrigerating or freezing. Keeps in fridge for 10 days. Freezer for 6-months.

This is one of my husbands and my daughter's, favorite Saturday morning treats. This is also another great use for the Focaccia Flatbread recipe, but store-bought whole-grain mini-pizza dough can be used.

Breakfast Pizza

I made the dough for individual use – 8" or less.

Marinara or Pizza Sauce
3-eggs (1-per person)
1-c fresh chopped parsley or basil, optional

Parmesan or Pecorino Cheese
6 Slices Prosciutto or leftover Chicken

Preheat oven to 425. Stoneware works best for this. Place the stone in the oven, while preheating to get it hot. Roll out dough to desired size and place on heated baking sheet. Spread small amount of marinara, leaving a 1" border to prevent run-off. Place the slices of prosciutto, leaving a space in the center for the egg. Crack egg into a bowl first (to ensure it doesn't break). Pour into center of ham and bake 25-30 minutes until dough is light brown and egg is set. Remove and top with cheese and parsley.

Fresh spinach can be added under the prosciutto. Serve immediately.

Brussels Bruschetta

1 lb. Brussels sprouts, halved
¾ c purple cabbage
1 c fresh parsley
¼ c white balsamic vinegar
6 fresh thyme sprigs

1 carrot, rough chopped
2 celery stalks, rough chopped
1 c dried cranberries
1 orange, zested & juiced
4 Tbsp. extra virgin olive oil

4-slices of prosciutto **OR** 5-slices of genoa salami, *optional*

In food processor, add the cabbage, carrot, celery, halved Brussels, parsley and leaves from thyme sprigs. Pulse until confetti consistency. Transfer to large mixing bowl; add the orange zest, juice and dried cranberries, toss to combine. In a large sauté pan over medium-high heat, add the oil. and cook, stirring occasionally. Add the balsamic vinegar, salt and pepper. Continue to cook until tender and cranberries are plump.

Notes:
 ➢ Toast thin slices of whole-grain crostini, top with a few pieces of chopped salami and a spoon of the Brussels mixture and serve as an appetizer
 ➢ It can be served warm or room temp as a salad. Lightly bake the salami OR prosciutto. Break into pieces over the top of the salad and serve
 ➢ Instead of bread, it can be served in endive leaves, lettuce or collard leaf wraps. The cured meat can be added or omitted
 ➢ It can be served as a cold salad from the start and not cooked at all

Brussels Sprouts Salad

1 lb. Fresh Brussels sprouts
2 celery stalk
4-5 Epazote leaves *(see note)*
2 tsp. red wine vinegar
2 Tbsp. dried parsley
Salt and pepper to taste

5 radish
2 Green onion – *optional*
1 lemon – zested & juiced
¾ c canola oil, grapeseed or olive oil
1 Tbsp. dried oregano

Wash, dry and trim ends of Brussels sprouts. Halve and place in food processor. Process until confetti consistency and place in large bowl. Roughly chop the radish, celery and if using, green onion and Epazote leaves. Process and add to bowl. Add all remaining ingredients and stir well to combine.

Refrigerate for 30 minutes for flavors to fully develop. Stir well before serving, taste and readjust if necessary. Fresh herbs make this dish even more delicious and refreshing. Fresh herb measurements are as follows: Parsley ½ c – ¾ c. Oregano ½ c

NOTE: Epazote is a fresh herb used in Latin cooking for reducing the effect of flatulence. It is very mild in flavor. I use it when cooking or making bean salsas as well.

Butternut Squash Soup

1-peeled, seeded and chopped butternut squash
1-leek *(see note)*
1 celery stalk, chopped

1 carrot, chopped
1 sweet potato, chopped
1-box chicken or vegetable stock

Seasonings: Tsp. Cinnamon, ½ tsp. Cayenne pepper, salt, pepper, tsp. Coriander *(optional)*, tsp. Dried sage, 2-Tbsp. parsley, 2-Tbsp. basil and 2-bay leaves

In a heavy Dutch-oven style pot, drizzle small amount of Olive oil. Add all the chopped veggies and sauté until tender. Add seasonings and continue cooking until soft. Cover with stock and/or water. Stir to completely combine. Cover and cook over medium heat until soft enough to puree.

Puree options: *Remove Bay leaves prior to blending.* Hand-held immersion blender, food processor or traditional blender. *if using a traditional blender, be sure to cover the lid with a towel and hold firmly to ensure the hot liquid does not escape.*

☞ I start with a small amount of seasonings and readjust after it's purred.

Topping Options:
Cornbread croutons
Toasted pumpkin seeds

Tbsp. plain Greek yogurt
Diced green apple

Notes:
☞ Leeks must be cleaned properly or they are very gritty. Do not use the dark green part. Slice thin the base and place in a small bowl with cold water. Use fingers to separate. Let sit for a few minutes. The grit will fall to bottom of bowl. Fish out leeks with fingers and add to sauté. Onion may be substituted.
☞ Do not peel the sweet potato. This soup will be pureed and the skin adds extra nutrients.
☞ Fennel cubed is a great addition or substitute for celery. It has a better flavor and is great for digestion. Save the green fern tops in a baggie and add to salads or meatballs for additional flavor. Can also be used to make tea. Just place some fennels greens in a cup, top with hot water, cover and steep for 5-minutes. Remove greens prior to drinking. Great for an upset tummy. ☺

By far and large, the MOST requested recipe I get is my bean dip. It is probably the most versatile, or at least runs a close second to Quinoa pesto. This is a great alternate to regular hummus.

Cannellini Bean Dip

15 oz. can cannellini beans, rinsed & drained
1-lemon, zested & juiced
Salt and pepper to taste
¼ c Olive, grapeseed **or** canola oil

1 garlic clove
1 c fresh parsley
½ tsp. dried oregano and basil

Place all ingredients in a food processor. Blend until smooth consistency. Scrape side, blend again if needed. Remove to covered container and refrigerate for at least 30 minutes prior to service.

Serving options: Any fresh veggies _(endive leaves, celery, fennel, peppers, carrot)_, whole-grain or gluten-free crackers, bagel chips, pita crisps, multi-grain or blue-corn Tostitos

Notes:
- ➤ Can be topped with crumbled bacon as well.
- ➤ 2 tbsp. of tahini can be added to make into hummus.
- ➤ A variety of beans are an option, with the exception of dark colored beans _(red or black)_. These tend to give a poor end appearance.
- ➤ This is also great used as a spread for sandwiches or wraps in place of mayo
- ➤ Garlic is optional

Chicken and Black Bean Soup

Any leftover chicken breast or thighs (no skin), cut into chunks

2 celery stalks, chopped

1 garlic clove, minced

1 – can black beans, drained/rinsed

1 onion, chopped

1 bell pepper, chopped

1-box low-sodium chicken broth

Seasonings: tsp. cumin, bay leaf, tbsp. dried oregano, salt/pepper, ½ tsp. paprika, hot pepper seeds to taste

In Dutch oven or large pan, over medium-high heat, add 2-Tbsp. olive oil. Sauté all veggies until tender. Stirring occasionally. Add beans, chicken and all seasonings. Add enough broth to cover. Heat through. Taste and readjust if necessary.

I always have leftover chicken or turkey. I cook with it so much that I usually buy the whole carcass; it's more economical and I can use the bones to make homemade stock and freeze. This was a very quick meal to use up leftovers.

To increase nutrients, just before serving, add handful of chopped dark leafy greens (spinach, collard or Swiss chard). Cooked quinoa or brown rice can be added also; if using however, add the grain to the bowl, then top with the soup. I do not store any grain in the soup, it swells too much and becomes flavorless.

Chicken Minestrone

3 chicken breasts, skinless, cubed	1 c brown rice (or Quinoa)
½ c – 1 c dark red kidney beans, drained & rinsed	2 celery stalk, diced
15 oz. can diced tomatoes	1 c chicken broth

Seasonings: 4 fresh basil leaves chopped, 2 handfuls fresh parsley chopped, salt/pepper, hot pepper flakes, 1 bay leaf

1 small onion, diced	1 carrot, diced
2 Tbsp. tomato paste	1 garlic clove, minced
½ c red wine	1 sm. Head of collard greens, chopped

Cook rice or quinoa first and let cool. In large sauté pan, add 2-Tbsp. olive oil and sauté chicken until golden brown. Add chopped onion, carrot, celery and garlic. Season w/salt, pepper, bay leaf and hot pepper flakes if using. Add tomato paste, diced tomatoes, wine and broth. Stir to combine. Cover and simmer for 20 minutes. If it gets too thick, thin out with water to desired consistency. Just before serving, add the chopped collard greens and beans and let warm through.

Serve over quinoa or brown rice, top with chopped herbs, tbsp. Greek yogurt and/or parmesan cheese.

Chicken-Zucchini Quinoa Poppers

1 lb. ground chicken
2 Tbsp. fresh chives, minced
4-sprigs fresh thyme, minced
½ c cooked, cooled quinoa

2 c grated zucchini
¼ c fresh parsley, minced
salt, pepper

☞*Cook's note*: After zucchini is grated, be sure to squeeze out excess water. A ricer can be used if available.

Preheat oven 400. Mix altogether by hand and form mini-sized meatballs. Place poppers on a sil-pat or parchment lined baking sheet and bake for 25 minutes. Let cool slightly prior to serving.

Serving options: Fresh, raw salsa, homemade guacamole or my herb-yogurt feta dip!

Chicken Waldorf Salad

Ingredients:

2 green apples cored & chopped

½ c shredded or cubed cooked chicken

1/3 c chopped cucumber

½ c chopped fresh fennel (celery can be
  substituted)

½ c chopped walnuts

½ c grapes, halved

1/3 c chopped red or green onion

Seasonings:

2 heaping tbsp. of Greek yogurt

½ of an orange or lemon zested & juiced

Salt, pepper, tbsp. dried

1 heaping tbsp. of Mayo

Tsp or so of extra virgin olive oil

Tsp. of Agave or Tbsp. of Honey

Place all ingredients in a bowl. Add seasonings; stir well to combine. Cover and refrigerate for at least 30-minutes before serving. Toss again and taste for adjustments if necessary.

Notes:

- ⑥ Remove skin from chicken and season with anise seeds, coriander, salt and pepper before cooking. Cool completely before adding to salad
- ⑥ Any apples and any citrus can be used
- ⑥ If using fresh parsley, use 1 c chopped
- ⑥ If using the fresh fennel, add ¼ c chopped fern leaves

My good friend Debbie Stevenski, gave me the idea for this recipe. She had a version of this recipe that I tweaked to make it my own. I've learned so much from her; she's as passionate, if not, more so than I am about Health and Wellness. I'm very thankful for her willingness to share her wisdom.

Cranberry and Pomegranate Dip

1 pkg. fresh cranberries
1 c pomegranate juice
Orange, zested & juiced
4 oz. Greek, plain yogurt

½ c red wine, optional
½ c sugar
4 oz. mascarpone cheese
½ tsp. cinnamon

In a medium size sauce pan, add cranberries, pomegranate juice, wine, orange zest and juice and stir to combine. Bring to a boil, stirring occasionally. Reduce heat to low. Once cranberries start to pop, taste for desired sweetness. Turn off and allow to cool. Add the cheese, yogurt and cinnamon and blend w/ handheld immersion to a smooth consistency.

I like to serve this with toasted whole-grain pita cut into triangles. This is a lighter, healthier option to make during the holidays and the color just pops!

Creamy Broccoli Salad

1 Carrot
½ lb. fresh broccoli heads
1/3 c dried cranberries
1 celery stalk

½ lemon
1 granny smith apple
¼ c walnuts

Dressing: ½ c mayo, ¾ c plain, non-fat Greek yogurt, 2 Tbsp. olive oil, 1-tsp each of dried parsley and basil, ¼ tsp. dried thyme, 1/8 tsp. each of cinnamon and nutmeg, salt and pepper

Rough chop all the veggies, apple and walnuts; place into large mixing bowl. Zest and juice half of lemon into bowl and add cranberries.

In a separate bowl, mix the dressing. Add to salad and stir well to combine. Let refrigerate for flavors to combine. Taste and readjust if necessary.

- ½ fresh orange may be substituted for lemon
- Pistachios or almonds may be substituted for walnuts
- Can be served alone or in a Swiss chard, romaine, endive or collard leaf to make a wrap
- Diced cooked chicken may be added
- ¼ c minced purple onion may be added

Broccoli contains sulforaphane, rich in antioxidants and has anti-cancer properties. It helps boost immune systems. Best eaten raw rather than cooked for maximize nutrient intake.

Dijon-Vinaigrette

¼ c Dijon mustard
1 whole lime, zested & juiced
Tsp. each of dried parsley, basil and oregano
1 ¼ c oil

2 hefty pinches of sea salt
¼ c to ½ c chopped fresh tomato
Pinch Pepper

Using a blender, add all ingredients _except_ oil. Start blender slowly drizzle in the oil while still running.

- ✞ Fresh herbs are also an option. Just start with a Tbsp. of each and increase to your liking
- ✞ The tomato is optional. I like to add it for color and its juices lend a lot of flavor

Makes: 1 ½ cups. Store in sealed container in refrigerator for up to 5-days.

Easter Bread

Makes 4-small braided loaves

1 ½ c gluten-free flour blend	4-5 c white flour
3 Tbsp. olive oil	2 eggs
¼ c coconut sugar	½ c almond or goat milk
¾ c water	2 pkg. yeast
1-orange, zested & juiced	2 Tbsp. raw honey
Tbsp. anise extract	3 tbsp. Anise seed

Whisk together flours with tbsp. salt and anise seed; set aside. Warm milk in saucepan; add sugar and oil, whisk to melt. Zest and juice the orange into the warm ¾ c water; add honey, yeast and extract. Let activate 5 minutes. In separate bowl, beat eggs with small amount of goat or almond milk. Using stand mixer, add milk mixture, yeast mixture and eggs. Start machine running and slowly add flour mixture. Allow to knead on low-medium speed until dough pulls away from sides and starts to form around dough hook. Additional flour may be needed. Oil a large bowl, transfer dough and turn to coat. Cover and allow to raise 2-3 hours.

Form into loaves, braided or not. Brush tops with beaten egg and sprinkle w/coconut sugar. Bake on 375 for 20-30 minutes, rotating if needed to color evenly.

I know what you're thinking, an egg salad recipe, really? Yes, it's an underrated dish; a great place to hide lots of veggies, greens, high in protein and versatile not to mention filling.

Egg Salad

6-hardboiled eggs
2 celery stalks
½ c carrot
½ c sugar snap peas

½ turnip
½ c radish
½ c spinach

Seasonings: ½ c Greek non-fat yogurt, 1/3 c mayo, Tbsp. Dijon, 2 Tbsp. dried parsley, 1- tbsp. dried dill, salt/pepper, Tbsp. dried basil, tsp. coriander

I use a food processor to mince all veggies and process the eggs last. I like a confetti style salad, but everything can be cut by hand to desired shape/size.

Add chopped items to bowl with all seasonings. Stir well to combine and keep covered and refrigerated no longer than 5-days.

➢ Great on an open faced sandwich. Toasted Ezekiel bread, slices of mayo, avocado, onion, topped w/arugula and a slice of cooked pancetta
➢ Great served in any type of lettuce leaf with some chopped chicken or turkey

Eggplant Bruschetta

2 Japanese eggplant   Roasted Red Pepper Dip (see page 40)

Bruschetta *(any type)* I make my own with tomatoes, garlic, celery and seasonings

Seasonings: salt/pepper, olive oil

Slice eggplant lengthwise, season with salt, pepper and olive oil. Using a hot grill pan, sear the slices on each side. Remove and let cool. Top each slice with bruschetta and Tbsp. of red pepper dip, serve immediately.

Prep options:

  ➤ Yellow or green zucchini can be substituted for eggplant
  ➤ Hollowed out cucumbers can be used for a raw option
  ➤ Increase protein by adding cooked, cooled, cubed chicken or turkey

I created this recipe for Mother's Day 2015. My sister-in-law, Inez and I were making a mother's day dinner to honor our mother-in-law, Sherry. Sherry loves to try new things and she is very adventurous when it comes to food.

Gazpacho!

2 Fresh tomatoes – chopped
1 red bell pepper – seeded & chopped
1 garlic
½ lemon *(zest & juice)*
¼ c each fresh parsley, basil, oregano

Salt /Pepper to taste
jalapeno – seeded & chopped *(optional)*
½ of carrot - peeled & chopped
1 celery stalk
2 Tbsp. olive oil

In food processor, blend all vegetables well until smooth. Season with juice, salt, pepper, oil and herbs; process again. Refrigerate for at least 45 minutes for flavors to marry. Taste and readjust seasonings if necessary. Serve cold.

Topping options: Hardboiled eggs, grilled shrimp or poultry, croutons, minced chives, Tostitos, diced cucumbers and tsp. plain Greek yogurt, chopped cilantro or parsley

Goat Cheese Dip

Makes 1-cup

5 oz Chavrie goat cheese
1 c fresh parsley, minced
½ c plain Greek, non-fat yogurt
¼ tsp. each dried basil, parsley, oregano & dill

½ lime, zested & juiced
salt, pepper to taste
½ tsp. Dijon

Whisk all ingredients together until thoroughly combined. Chill 20 minutes for flavors to combine. Taste & readjust if necessary.

Uses:

- ☞ Serve on creamed soups/chili
- ☞ Use in place of sour cream in fajita's or wraps
- ☞ Use as dip with veggies, Tostitos or beet chips
- ☞ Use as spread for collard & Swiss wraps or sandwiches

I created this recipe for an away game when my daughter was playing high school soccer. I wanted to provide some healthier options to what they would give the girls during long road trips. Due to the nature of ingredients, it's very important to ensure there are no food allergy or restrictions. This is high in fiber but also in sugar, so it is good for athletes or for eating during or after long cycling trips or after a high intensity cardio as a recovery.

Granola
Makes 7-cups

3 c- Oats
½ c dried cranberries
1/3 c pine nuts
¾ c dark brown sugar
½ c walnuts, chopped

1/3 c almonds, chopped
1/3 c wheat germ
½ c dried blueberries
1/3 c sunflower seeds
1 Tbsp. sesame seeds

Spices: ½ tsp. cayenne pepper, 1 tsp. chili powder, salt/pepper, ¼ tsp. nutmeg and ginger, Tbsp. cinnamon

Preheat oven to 350. In a large bowl, toss all ingredients together. Beat together 2-egg whites w/2 Tbsp. agave nectar and add to bowl, along with seasonings. Toss well to ensure everything is coated.

Spread out on large baking sheet. I used a silicone sheet to keep everything from sticking. Drizzle the top with olive oil and bake for 35-40 minutes. Depending on oven type, you may want to pull and stir half-way through the cooking time to ensure even browning.

Freezes well.

Grape leaves Stuffed with Quinoa Pesto

1-recipe of Quinoa Pesto
Kalamata olives, to garnish
Feta cheese crumbles, to garnish

Grape leaves, drained & rinsed
(Peloponnese brand)

In colander, drain, separate and rinse grape leaves; pat dry

Begin rolling: Place tsp. of quinoa in center of leaf. Fold lower section up first, then sides. *(burrito style).*

Plate the stuffed grape leaves. Top with salt, pepper, olive oil, fresh lemon juice, feta crumbles and serve.

☞ Cabbage leaves can be substituted for grape leaves.
☞ Collard green leaves can also be used.

I made these 2-ways. Raw and Baked after prepped. I liked them raw, my hubby and a few family members preferred them baked. I encourage you to try them both ways.

This is a great way to use up leftover quinoa pesto and seriously increase some nutrients with trying the Grape Leaves; which are high in potassium vitamin A, and fiber

Grapefruit, Fennel and Herb Salad

1 – grapefruit, segmented *(save juice for dressing)*

1 fresh fennel bulb, thinly sliced

1 celery stalk, cut on the diagonal

½ of carrot, shaved w/veggie peeler

Seasonings: 4-5 sprigs of fennel ferns, 5 fresh basil leaves, 1 small bunch of fresh mint leaves, 3-4 sprigs of fresh chives, 2-Tbsp. olive oil, salt, pepper, Pecorino cheese shaved to top, optional

Dressing: Juice from grapefruit, 2-tbsp olive oil, salt, pepper – whisk to combine

Place all ingredients in a large bowl, top with dressing and stir well to coat and combine. Just before serving, top with a few slices of shaved pecorino or parmesan cheese

Greek Quinoa

1 c quinoa (tri-color)
1-garlic clove
½ c cherry tomatoes, quartered
½ c Kalamata olives, chopped

1 cup chicken broth
1" cube fresh ginger, peeled
¼ c pepperoncini's, minced
1/3 c Feta cheese crumbles

Seasonings: salt, pepper, ½ lemon zested, tsp. dried parsley, oregano and coriander, ½ tsp. thyme, ¼ c olive oil

Place 1-cup broth, ginger cube and garlic clove in medium-sized saucepan, bring to boil. Add quinoa, reduce to low, cover and simmer 10 minutes. Discard garlic & ginger; transfer cooled quinoa to large mixing bowl. Add all remaining ingredients and seasonings. Stir well to combine. Cover and refrigerate 30 minutes; taste and readjust if necessary.

Prep options:

- Minced cucumbers can be added
- Fresh herbs can be substituted
- Great served on grilled veggies, fish or chicken
- Use as dip with Tostitos, veggies or in wraps
- Add to collard leaf or pita wraps with cooked diced chicken

Another recipe I get a lot of requests for is my *Herbed Feta and Greek Yogurt Dip*. It is a healthy alternative to Ranch dressing. Once I was no longer able to consume dairy, I had to find ways to enjoy similar foods. This recipe is great for kids. Most kids love ranch and this is a much healthier, unprocessed, no sugar recipe. Great way to use up fresh herbs as well.

Herbed Feta and Greek Yogurt Dip

½ c fresh parsley, minced
½ c mayo
Tsp. each dried oregano & basil
Salt and pepper to taste
1 lemon *(zested & juiced)*

1 Tbsp. course mustard or Dijon
1 c plain, non-fat Greek yogurt
½ tsp. coriander, *optional*
1/3 c feta cheese crumbles, *optional*

Place all ingredients in bowl and whisk well to combine. Cover and refrigerate for at least 30 minutes prior to service.

Serving options: fresh veggies, multi-grain or blue-corn Tostitos

Notes:

➢ This is also great used as a spread to sandwiches, wraps or pita's.
➢ Crumbled bacon can also be added to the top prior to service
➢ This can be made Taziki style by adding chopped cucumber and minced fresh dill
➢ This is a very healthy replacement to ranch-style dips.
➢ Remember to serve and keep cold. Chill bowl prior to service.
➢ Can be made Mexican with chili powder, paprika and cumin

June 27, 2013

Every fall, I harvest my herb garden and create infused oils. I had 1-left that I hadn't used over the winter so I have been trying to create dishes to use it up before making more this fall. I infused canola oil with jalapeño peppers and hot pepper seeds to make *hot pepper oil*. This is optional. Regular oil can be used in this dish; however, I was going for HOT. My husband loves hot and spicy food and I rarely get it hot enough for him. I hit the target with this dish though – his eyes were watering and hiccups followed shortly. This is a great dish to use up leftover taco shells.

Hot & Spicy Taco Soup Shooters!

15 oz. can diced tomatoes	7 oz. can chipotle peppers in adobo sauce
1 garlic clove	½ onion
12 oz bottle of dark beer	Jalapeno oil *(or canola, olive oil or grapeseed)*
Greek Yogurt to top	4-5 taco shells *(broken into pieces)* or Tostitos

Seasonings: 1-Tsp. Salt, ½ tsp. Cayenne, ½ tsp. Chili powder,1/4 tsp. Cumin, ¼ tsp. Turmeric, & 1-bay leaf

Use food processor to finely mince onion and garlic. In a large sauté pan, sauté the minced veggies in oil with salt, pepper and a bay leaf. Add the diced tomatoes, peppers and ½ bottle of dark beer. Bring to a simmer, stirring occasionally. Add the remaining spices and simmer for about 15 minutes. If the mixture gets too thick, add water.

Transfer mixture to a blender and add remaining beer and the broken taco shells or chips. Process until completely smooth. Mixture should be thick.

I served the soup in small shot glasses with a spoon of Greek Yogurt and broken taco shell pieces.

During the winter months, I always make a cooked version of salsa since ingredients and herbs are not as accessible. It has multiple uses and adds so much flavor and texture to just about anything. Lycopene, found in tomatoes, is only released when they are cooked; it has anti-inflammatory benefits.

Italian Salsa
Cooked

14.5 oz. can fire roasted tomatoes
1 garlic clove, minced
2-celery stalks, minced
½ c cherry tomatoes, chopped

1/3 c minced onion
1 carrot, minced
¼ c radish (2-3), minced
1 lime, zested & juiced

Seasonings: Tbsp. tomato paste, 2 bay leaves, ¼ c extra-virgin olive oil, salt, pepper, tsp. each dried basil and oregano, 2 tsp dried parsley, ½ tsp. dried dill and coriander

In large skillet, over medium-high heat, add the oil and all veggies. Cover and cook, stirring occasionally for 20 minutes. Add chicken broth or water to thin out if it gets too thick. Add all seasonings except for lime. Cover and cook additional 10 minutes, again adding liquid if too thick. Add lime and Tbsp. oil stir and serve.

Remove and discard bay leaves before service. Best served warm

Notes:

- This is delicious for breakfast, lunch or dinner. Add warmed salsa to a ramekin, top with egg and bake until egg is set. Top w/grated pecorino cheese, blk pepper and serve with or without toasted Ezekiel or Gluten-free bread
- Baked pancetta can be added under the egg before baking.

Leek & Fennel Soup

3 leeks, sliced and stems discarded

1 carrot, chopped

1 celery stalk, chopped

3 c chicken or vegetable broth

2-Tbsp. olive oil

1 fennel bulb, sliced thin

¼ onion, chopped

1 potato, chopped

2-3 c water

Seasonings: 2-sprigs fresh rosemary, tsp. dried sage, basil, thyme and parsley, Salt/Pepper to taste

Add all veggies to a large stock pot with oil over medium-high heat. Sauté until tender. Add all seasonings and continue to cook for 10 minutes. Add the broth and water. Bring to boil, reduce heat. Stir occasionally for 30 minutes. Once all veggies are tender, puree soup to velvety consistency.

Prep options:

➢ Hand-held immersion blender may be used or Regular blender

➢ Can be served topped with a Tbsp. plain Greek yogurt

➢ Freezes well

Mushroom and Greens Frittata

Makes 18 pieces (depending on cut)

Ingredients:

3 c greens
10 Brussels sprouts (1 cup), *optional*
1 c fresh parsley leaves, no stems
3 eggs

¼ of an onion, rough chopped
5 baby bella mushrooms, quartered
½ c leftover pre-cooked protein, *optional*
¼ c goat milk

Seasonings:

Salt/Pepper, 2 Tbsp. olive oil, ½ tsp. dried oregano & basil, ¼ tsp. turmeric

Using a food processor, add all veggies. May have to be done in 2-batches. Scrape sides to ensure everything is finely ground. In a 12" skillet, over medium-high heat, add the oil. Once hot, add the veggies and protein. Sauté, stirring occasionally for 12 minutes. In a bowl, beat the eggs with milk. Spread the veggie/protein mixture evenly around the bottom of pan. Pour the egg/milk mixture all around and let set-up for 5-6 minutes. Bubbles will start to form in center. Gently, run a spatula around outside to loosen. Place under broiler for 3-4 minutes, just to set the top & lightly brown. Remove and let cool before transferring to cutting board.

Notes:

- ⑥ Brussels sprouts are optional. If using, remove the ends and cut in half prior to adding to food processor
- ⑥ Any pre-cooked protein can be added (chicken breast or turkey breast cut into cubes, or ground meats)
- ⑥ Any low-fat milk can be used (almond, or cow's milk)
- ⑥ Any dark greens can be used (kale, collards, Swiss chard, spinach). Must be fresh, not frozen or canned
- ⑥ If mixture gets dry while cooking, add additional oil. Mushrooms are like sponges and tend to soak up quickly
- ⑥ Keep an eye on it once in the broiler. It can burn easily depending on type of heat and closeness to broiler

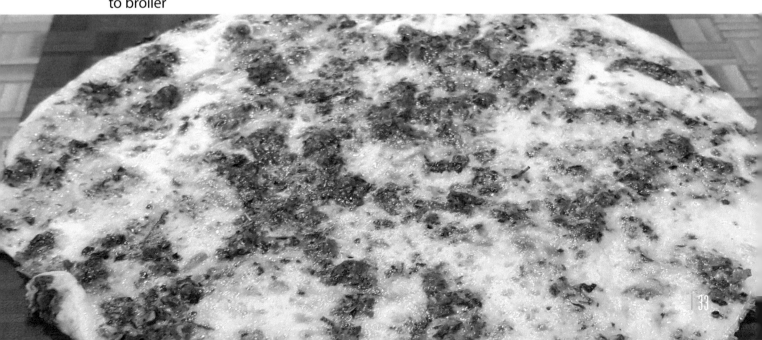

Pea Pesto

1-cup frozen peas, thawed   ½ c lima beans
½ c fresh mint   ½ c fresh parsley
1 lemon; zested & juiced   ¼ c grapeseed or canola oil
Salt, pepper   ¼ tsp. dried oregano

Pulse all ingredients together in a food processor. Refrigerate for 15-20 minutes to marry flavors. Taste and readjust.

Notes

- ⑥ Lima beans are optional. I add them to increase nutrients and balance the sweetness of the peas
- ⑥ Serve in Belgium endive leaves, bell peppers, celery, fennel, salami crisps or crostini and top with chopped walnuts or crispy prosciutto

Poppy Seed Vinaigrette

Makes ¾ c

1-orange & 1-lemon (*zested & juiced*)
¾ c olive/canola oil
2 tsp. Dijon
½ tsp. each of dried basil, parsley and oregano

Tbsp. poppy seeds
Tsp. sea salt
1 tsp. apple cider vinegar

In small bowl, whisk together all ingredients until combined. A Nutri-bullet or blender can also be used.

➢ Grapeseed oil may be substituted for canola or olive oil

Pumpkin Soup

1 small baking pumpkin
1 fennel bulb, chopped
½ onion
4" piece of peeled ginger root
32 oz. chicken or veg broth

1 celery stalk, chopped
2 carrots, chopped
1 orange bell pepper, chopped
2 Tbsp. olive oil

Seasonings: Salt, Pepper, 1 bay leaf, 2-sprigs fresh thyme, 1-sprig fresh rosemary, 1 c fresh parsley, 7-fresh basil leaves, ¼ tsp. coriander and cinnamon, pinch of nutmeg and cayenne pepper

Prep pumpkin first. Halve and remove seeds. Drizzle with olive oil, salt and pepper and roast at 420 flesh side down for 25 minutes. Let cool. Remove outer peel. The pumpkins seeds can be roasted and spiced for use in soup or eaten separately.

In food processor, add chopped vegetables and puree. Heat olive oil in dutch oven over medium-high heat. Add the vegetables and sauté until tender about 10 minutes. Add the pumpkin flesh, broth, bay, thyme, rosemary, parsley and stir well to combine. Cover and stir frequently for 25 minutes. Remove the twigs, add the basil leaves and puree with handheld mixer or transfer to blender.

Add remaining seasonings, stir and serve. Taste and readjust if necessary.

Serving options: Roasted pumpkin seeds, pomegranate seeds, chevre goat cheese or pistachios.

- ⑥ This dish goes great with dill flavored grilled chicken thighs
- ⑥ This dish freezes well
- ⑥ Toasted crostini with drizzled honey accompanies this well
- ⑥ I'm sure canned pumpkin could be substituted but I didn't try it

Purple Passion

¼ of whole purple cabbage
1-orange, zested & juiced
1-granny smith apple

1-whole raw, beet
1-lemon, zested & juiced

Seasonings: Salt, Pepper, Tbsp. canola oil

In food processor, shred each separately. Cabbage, then beet, then apple. Transfer each to a large mixing bowl. Add the zests and juice of the orange and lemon, season with salt, pepper, oil and toss well to thoroughly combine.

Cover and refrigerate. Once it marinates, taste and readjust if necessary.

This dish can also be sautéed for 15 minutes and served warm.

Quinoa Pesto

½ c cooked & cooled quinoa
1 c fresh parsley
1 celery, diced
1 shallot, optional
¼ c grapeseed or olive oil
2 Tsp. dried oregano & basil
1 garlic clove, *optional*

1 c arugula
1 c kale and collard greens
1 small diced tomato
1 small green onion
salt and pepper to taste
pinch of celery salt, *optional*
½ lemon or lime, zested & juiced

Place quinoa in large bowl. In a food processor, add parsley, garlic, kale, collard greens, shallot, green onion, citrus and oil. Pulse until finely minced and add to quinoa bowl. Add diced celery, tomato, herbs, and seasonings. Stir well to combine. Cover and refrigerate 30 minutes. Taste and readjust seasonings, if needed.

Serving options: fresh veggies, whole-grain or gluten-free crackers, bagel chips, pita crisps, multi-grain or blue-corn Tostitos

Note:

- ➢ Condiment or side dish to fresh grilled fish, chicken or turkey
- ➢ Add to leave or grain wraps and pita sandwiches
- ➢ Add spice with cayenne, red pepper flakes or minced jalapeno.
- ➢ Quinoa is a great substitute for bulgur wheat in Tabbouleh recipes
- ➢ Grated pecorino or parmesan can be added to be more of a traditional pesto
- ➢ Cook quinoa in veg or chicken broth to increase flavor/nutrients

Raspberry Vinaigrette

Makes ¾ c

1 c raspberries *(thawed or fresh)*
Zest & juice of 1-lime & 1-orange
¼ c canola or safflower oil

1 Tbsp. honey
1 Tbsp. agave nectar

Add all ingredients to a blender or nutra-bullet. Process until smooth. Pour through a fine mesh sieve to separate seeds from dressing.

Place in sealed container. Keep refrigerated for 5-days.

Roasted Pepper Dip

3-4 roasted red peppers, jarred *(see prep note)   ¼ c mayo
½ c Greek, plain non-fat yogurt   ½ lemon, zested

Seasonings: salt/pepper, 1-c fresh parsley, ½ tsp. dried oregano, basil and dill, pinch of dried thyme

In food processor, combine all ingredients and blend until smooth consistency; scrape sides and blend again.

Cover and refrigerate for 30 minutes to thicken/set. Keeps 7-days.

Prep notes/Options:

- ⑥ Be sure to pat-dry the peppers before adding to processor or it will make the dressing too wet
- ⑥ This can be served as a dip with vegetables, Tostitos, even Gluten-free crackers
- ⑥ Great as a spread for collard leaf wraps, whole-grain wraps or pita bread sandwiches
- ⑥ Use as a topping for bruschetta or for grilled chicken or tilapia

Tomato Basil Soup

28 oz can whole tomatoes
1 bay leaf
3 garlic cloves
2-cup fresh basil
Salt, Pepper, pinch dried oregano
½ c vegetable broth

1 tbsp. tomato paste
½ white onion
1 cup fresh cherry tomatoes
1 lemon – juiced
oil to sauté veggies

Rough chop the onion and garlic. Sauté gently over med-high heat in olive oil. Just enough oil to coat pan. Add bay leaf, salt and pepper

Once veggies are soft. Add the paste and cook until thoroughly combined. Add whole and fresh tomatoes, veg broth and cover. Simmer over medium heat for 30 minutes. Stir occasionally.

Remove from heat. Using a handheld immersion blender or regular blender, add the fresh basil, oregano and start blending to desired consistency. Stir in fresh lemon juice. Serve warm with desired toppings.

Topping options: Polenta croutons, herbed yogurt, parmesan cheese and crispy pancetta.

Turkey Waldorf Loaf

2 ½ lbs. ground turkey
1 carrot
1 Tbsp. ground fennel
1 ½ c dried cranberries
½ onion
1 celery

1 egg
1 c fresh parsley
Salt/Pepper
1 c nuts (any combo of *almonds, pistachios, walnuts*)

Preheat oven 365. In a large bowl, place ground turkey, cranberries and egg. In food processor, finely process remaining ingredients, add to turkey. Using hands, thoroughly mix together.

On a baking sheet lined with parchment or sil-pat, form the loaf to desired thickness and length. Bake 45 minutes

➢ I make this particular recipe as an appetizer with the following: 3 apples, cored and cut into cubes, 1-orange zested & juiced, ¼ tsp. cinnamon, pinch nutmeg and red and green grapes.

➢ Let the meatloaf refrigerate prior to cutting into cubes for the skewers. The colder it is, the easier and more accurate it cuts. Place an apple piece, 1-grape and a 1-cube of the loaf onto a skewer and serve with the Herbed Yogurt Mayo recipe.

➢ This recipe makes a lot of meatloaf. It can be frozen for later use, used for sandwiches or served as a main course. It can also be cubed and tossed all together with the apples and grapes as a salad.

Yogurt Coleslaw

1-sm head cabbage
1-carrot
1 fennel bulb, *optional*

3 celery stalks
1 small bunch chives

Seasonings: 1 orange zested & juiced, Tsp. apple cider vinegar, Tbsp. dried parsley, basil and Dijon, ¼ c mayo, 1/3 c Greek plain non-fat yogurt, salt/pepper, Tbsp. grapeseed oil and agave nectar

I use a food processor to make confetti style cabbage. If you do not have a processor, all veggies can be cut to desired texture. If using processor, rough chop all the veggies in large chunks and process a little at a time, transferring to large bowl.

Add all seasonings and stir well to combine thoroughly. Once it marinates in refrigerator, it will make more juices. Cover and keep cold for 30 minutes before adjusting seasonings.

➢ Any cabbages may be combined (purple, Napa). Makes more colorful ☺

Served on top of turkey or chicken burgers is delish!

MINI-SIDES:

(Sauté's, Side-Dishes)

Artichoke & Olive Sauté

1 box (9 oz.) frozen artichokes
1 c fresh broccoli, optional
1 celery stalk, minced
1 cup Kalamata olives, chopped
Salt, Pepper to taste

½ fresh tomato, diced
½ onion, minced
½ lemon zested & juiced
tbsp. olive oil
Tsp. dried parsley, oregano & basil

Artichokes can be thawed first but they don't have to be. Over medium-high heat, sauté all ingredients until fork tender but still firm. Add broccoli towards the end to ensure it doesn't turn brown.

Serving options:

➤ Omit the broccoli and olives and this can be turned into a pesto in the food processor; add parmesan cheese. Can be tossed with short cut pasta, or served over toast crisps, in endive leaves or with fennel slices

➤ Cooked rice and chicken can be added to sauté to make a main course

BBQ Cauliflower

1 head cauliflower, cored & cut	2-limes, zested & juiced
1" fresh ginger root, grated	3 Tbsp. Dijon
3 Tbsp. Worcestershire	½ to 1 tsp. cayenne pepper
2 tsp. smoked paprika	3 Tbsp. agave nectar
2 Tsp. dried thyme	1 ½ tsp. coriander
3 tbsp. olive oil	

Preheat oven to 400 degrees. Cut cauliflower into bite size pieces, place in bowl. In separate bowl, whisk together all seasonings. Pour over cauliflower and toss well to thoroughly combine.

Placed on baking sheet; bake 30-35 minutes.

Prep options:

➢ Can be topped/served w/crispy pancetta

This is such a simple dish; the addition of anchovies increases nutrients, protein and flavor. They melt completely so you won't know they are in there. Great way to hide healthy stuff from kids.

Broccoli Sauté

1 lb. fresh broccoli	4 anchovy filets
½ c broth	½ tsp. dried oregano & basil
Salt/pepper to taste	5-Sundried tomatoes, *optional*
No oil needed	1 garlic clove minced, *optional*

Over medium high heat, add all ingredients and sauté for 5-8 minutes. Broccoli should maintain its green color.

Serving options:

➢ Can be transferred to a food processor and turned into broccoli pesto, just add some parmesan cheese. Toss with pasta, serve over toasted crostini, in endive leaves, or with celery or fennel slices
➢ Can be made spicy by adding hot pepper seeds or pinch of cayenne pepper
➢ Go easy on the salt; anchovies are naturally salty

Caponata!

1 eggplant, cubed	2 large tomatoes, cubed
2-hot peppers, rough chop	2-celery stalks, chopped
2 clove garlic, minced	1-yellow pepper, chopped
½ c Kalamta or green olives, pitted	1 –carrot, chopped
½ sweet onion, chopped	2 Tbsp. vinegar (cider or balsamic)
½ c broth (veg or chicken)	1" cube ginger, grated
½ c fresh mint & parsley	¼ c Olive oil

Seasonings: ¼ tsp. cumin and turmeric, ½ tsp. coriander and chili powder, pinch cinnamon, tsp. dried basil and oregano, salt and pepper

❖ Try and keep all vegetables about the same cut size, to ensure even cooking.

In a large sauté pan, heat olive oil. Toss in all vegetables and cook over medium-high heat for 10 minutes until they start to soften. Stir often. Add the broth and the seasonings and continue cooking until thoroughly combined and tender. Cook to desired consistency. I like texture and keeping the vegetables firm. I do not cook any longer than 20 minutes.

Notes:

➢ This accompanies turkey or chicken very well and is great added to wraps
➢ If spice isn't tolerable, omit the hot peppers
➢ Zucchini is a great substitute for eggplant
➢ Great as an appetizer on thin, crispy bread
➢ Can be used as leftover for beaten eggs in an omelet

Carrot and Sweet Potato Puree

2 carrots, peeled, chopped
2 celery stalk, chopped
1 garlic clove, minced
¼ c white wine
2 Tbsp. Greek plain yogurt

1 sweet potato, peeled, chopped
2 shallots, minced
1 ½" cube of fresh ginger, peeled
Chicken broth or water

Seasonings: Salt/pepper, Olive oil, 1-bay leaf, ½ tsp. red pepper flakes, Olive oil

In Dutch oven, over medium-high heat, add Tbsp. olive oil and all chopped veggies. Stir occasionally, about 10 minutes. Add bay leaf, seasonings and white wine. Continue cooking until tender. Additional liquid may need added

Once fork tender, remove from heat and add yogurt and puree with a handheld immersion blender or transfer to a stander blender and process until smooth.

- High fiber, great substitute for mashed potatoes – great Fall Color!
- Can be topped with grated Pecorino-Romano cheese

Cauliflower Puree

1 head cauliflower

1" ginger, peeled

¼ c parmesan or pecorino cheese

Seasonings: Salt, Pepper, 1 bay leaf, 3-4 sprigs fresh thyme, Tbsp. dried parsley, Tbsp. plain Greek yogurt, Tbsp. extra-virgin olive oil

Discard leaves/stems of cauliflower and break apart flowerets. Place in large pot along with sprigs of thyme, bay leaves and ginger root. Cover with water and lid; bring to boil. Simmer over medium heat, just until fork tender.

Drain and transfer to food processor. Discard steps of thyme & bay. Add all remaining seasonings and process until smooth consistency.

- 👍 For increased nutrients and sweeter flavor, cut and cube a sweet potato and add to water for cooking. Do not peel.
- 👍 ¼ c fresh parsley may be substituted for dry
- 👍 Can be topped w/minced chives and smoked paprika
- 👍 Can be topped with crispy pancetta or prosciutto

Creamy Turkey Sausage Sauté

5 oz. goat cheese
1 small tomato, diced
½ small onion, minced

1 ½ lb. sweet turkey sausage or plain ground turkey
2 celery stalks, diced

Seasonings: salt/pepper, tsp. dried parsley, oregano, basil

In large sauté pan, add the ground turkey or turkey sausage, minced vegetables and seasonings. Cook over medium-high heat, stirring occasionally until browned. Add the goat cheese and cook until melted and thoroughly combined.

Notes:

➢ If using turkey sausage links or in casings, be sure to remove meat from casing to cook
➢ If using plain turkey, add Tbsp. ground fennel seed to seasonings
➢ Can be topped w/crumbled blue corn Tostitos and Greek yogurt or guacamole
➢ Great served as taco-style salad w/dark greens and lots of vegetables

If you are going to try making bread, flatbread is a great place to start. It's quick, easy, requires no yeast. It can be flavored easily and has multiple uses once baked or grilled. Since I used Sun-dried tomatoes in the Kale Torta, I had them leftover and used them up in a pesto w/pistachios to top the grilled bread.

Focaccia Flatbread
(makes 2-3)

1 c water
1 c Gluten-free flour blend
salt/pepper
Tsp. dried oregano
Tsp. minced fresh rosemary

1 ¼ c flour
2 tsp. baking powder
2 Tbsp. olive oil
tsp. ground flaxseed

Preheat oven to 375. For the flatbread: in a stand mixer, with dough hook, add the flours, salt/pepper, oregano, flax, rosemary and baking powder. Start the machine, add the oil/water slowly. Allow to mix until forms a bowl. Wrap in parchment and refrigerate for 1-hour.

On a heavily floured surface, roll dough out to desired thickness and size. Dough will be sticky, so be sure and use plenty of flour to ensure it doesn't stick to countertop. A grill pan or gas grill can be used, to grill the dough or placed on stoneware and baked.

Top with any desired topping, cut and serve.

I part of this recipe to make the **Kale Torta** and the other Sun-dried tomato pesto as well as Avocado Cream and Cannellini Bean flatbread. I was able to multiple meals from 1-batch!

Be sure the gluten-free flour blend has high quality flours (*ex. quinoa, amaranth*)

Fruit Bruschetta

2 apples, cored & cubed

2 plums, cored & cubed

Havarti cheese

Handful of fresh Arugula or spinach

1 sm. White or purple onion, diced

1 baguette (whole wheat or gluten-free)

Extra Virgin Olive oil

Seasonings: salt, tsp. dried thyme and parsley, ½ tsp honey or agave nectar

In a large sauté pan, drizzle olive oil to coat. On medium high heat, add chopped fruits and onion. Stir occasionally, may need to add some water to help create the syrup. Add seasonings and continue to cook until tender but still firm.

Slice the baguette into ¼" pieces of crostini toasts. Place a tablespoon of fruit mixture, then greens if using, on each bread slice. Top with slice of cheese, bake at 400 until warm and cheese is melted. Serve immediately.

Options/Substitutions: Any apples can be used. Peaches can substitute plums. Any sharp white cheese (Fontina or Swiss).

Anytime I have leftovers, I love to make a Healthy Hash instead of using a bunch of starchy potatoes, I use good quality protein and veggies. Very filling and multiple uses

Healthy Hash

12 oz. Brussels sprouts
2 garlic cloves, minced
Tsp. anchovy paste, optional

1 c leftover bison, venison or beef
½ med. Onion, chopped
1-c cherry tomatoes

Seasonings: salt/pepper, tsp. each dried basil, oregano, parsley, 1 sprig fresh rosemary, hot pepper seeds optional, to add smoky flavor, include ½ tsp. paprika

Remove stems from Brussels and rough chop. In large skillet, add 2- tbsp. olive oil. Over medium-high heat, add garlic, onions, anchovy paste and tomatoes. Sauté until tender. Add Brussels and seasonings and ¼ c water to help soften. Cook over medium high heat, stirring occasionally just until tender. Greens should stay green.

➤ Great with scrambled eggs for breakfast
➤ Any cooked protein can be used
➤ Fresh kale or spinach may be added as well

Sneaky Turkey Sauté

½ c goat cheese

2 small sweet peppers

1-garlic clove

2 ½ c dark greens

Tbsp. Fennel seed, crushed

½ tsp. dried oregano, optional

½ onion

2 ½ lbs. ground turkey

1 c fresh parsley, optional

Salt and Pepper to taste

I didn't use any oil to sauté the turkey. It made enough juices on its own.

Over medium-high heat, brown the ground turkey. In food processor, finely grind all ingredients, except goat cheese. Add to cooked turkey with goat cheese and cook to thoroughly combine.

Serving options: Can be eaten alone, with cooked rice or topped with lettuce, tomato, olives, onion, Tostitos & yogurt. Delicious served in a large salad with sweet & sour dressing

Tabbouleh

1 c bulgur wheat, cooked & cooled

1 tomato, diced

1 garlic clove, minced

½ c pomegranate seeds, optional

½ cucumber, peeled & diced

½ c fresh corn

1 lemon, zested & juiced

Seasonings: 4-5 sprigs each of fresh oregano, chives, parsley and mint, rinse and diced, salt, pepper, ¼ c extra virgin olive oil

Combine all ingredients in a large bowl and toss well to combine. Cover and refrigerate for 30 minutes for flavors to marry. Taste and adjust if necessary.

> This can be made spicy with a minced jalapeno pepper
> Quinoa is a great, gluten-free substitute for bulgur wheat
> Great travel dish!
> Can be used in lettuce wraps with chopped cooked chicken for added protein and fresh spinach

MINI-MAINS DISHES

Beef Mini-Sliders w/Mushrooms & Onions

1 lb. ground beef, form 7-8 mini-patties, salt/pepper. In grill pan or outdoor grill, cook burgers to desired done-ness

Mushroom Reduction	**Caramelized Onions**
1 lb. Bella mushrooms, quartered	2 sm. White onions, sliced
½ oz. pkg. Dried porcini	1 garlic clove, minced
1 sprig fresh rosemary	1 sprig fresh rosemary
1-bay leaf	1-bay leaf
¼ tsp. red pepper flakes	½ c chicken broth
¼ tsp. cinnamon, chili powder	¼ tsp. anchovy paste
¼ tsp. cumin, coriander	½ tsp. vinegar
Pinch nutmeg	½ tsp. dried basil, oregano
½ c merlot	Tbsp. honey
Salt/Pepper	Salt/Pepper

Mushrooms: Sauté quartered mushrooms in olive oil over medium-high heat until they start to turn color. Additional oil may need to be added at first. Add remaining ingredients, stir, lower heat to medium and continue cooking until wine is evaporated and mushrooms are dark in color.

Onions: Sauté onions, garlic and ginger over medium heat in 2-Tbsp.olive oil. Season w/salt and pepper and continue cooking, stirring occasionally for 10 minutes. Add remaining ingredients and continue cooking, stirring occasionally for 12 minutes until liquid evaporates and onions are soft and caramelized.

Bison Chili

15 oz. can kidney beans, rinsed/drained
1 lb. ground bison
2 garlic clove
1 shallot, *optional*
12 oz. bottle beer *(corona)*
Tbsp. tomato paste

8 oz. tomato sauce
2 celery stalks
1 carrot
½ onion
¼ c veg or chicken broth

Seasonings: 1 oz. piece dark chocolate (70% or higher), Salt/Pepper, tsp. chili powder, ½ tsp. dried oregano, parsley, basil, ¼ tsp. turmeric, smoked paprika, dried thyme, coriander and cumin

In food processor, mince all veggies. In large Dutch oven, over medium-high heat, brown the bison w/tbsp. olive oil. Add the minced veggies and cook, stirring occasionally for 10 minutes. Add the tomato paste, beer, tomato sauce and dark chocolate. Stir until thoroughly combined and cook for 7 minutes. Add all seasonings and stir; reduce to medium-low heat and cook for 20-25 minutes to desired thickness. If too thick, add the ¼ c veg/chicken broth. Add kidney beans at the end, just to heat through

Notes/Variations:

- ☞ I serve with my Herbed Goat Cheese dip
- ☞ Beer can be substituted with broth
- ☞ Can be made spicy by adding a minced jalapeno or cayenne pepper
- ☞ Can be served with broken purple Tostito's

Cashew Chicken Wrap

1 whole-grain wrap
¼ c dried cranberries
Handful fresh spinach/arugula

¼ c granny smith apple, thinly sliced or small dice
½ c diced cooked & cooled chicken
Cashew butter

Lightly heat wrap in dry sauté pan or microwave. Spread cashew butter, thinly over base of wrap. Top with the diced chicken, cranberries, apples, and spinach. Fold sides over first, then roll up from base, burrito style. Cut and serve immediately.

➢ Whole-wheat, sun-dried tomato or gluten-free wrap can be used
➢ Collard leaf may be substituted for wrap
➢ Almond butter may be substituted for cashew butter
➢ Baby kale and or arugula can be added

Chicken "pizziaola" meatballs

Makes 22-24 meatballs

2 ½ - 3 lb. ground chicken
2 c fresh basil, minced
Salt, pepper
Tbsp. Dijon

8 oz. jar sun-dried tomatoes, drained and
   minced
1 cup fresh parsley (or 2 Tbsp. dried)
1 ½ c feta cheese crumbles

Mix together by hand, all ingredients, until thoroughly combined. Form into meatballs and bake at 375 for 45 minutes.

I serve with my Herbed Yogurt-Mayo.

Creamy, Quick Marinara

2 carrots

2 tbsp. tomato paste

¼ c Feta cheese

3 cloves garlic

14.5 oz. can tomatoes or tomato sauce

8 oz. water

Seasonings: 2-bay leaves, ½ tsp. each of salt, dried parsley & basil

Rough chop the carrots. Add all ingredients (*EXCEPT Feta*) to sauce pan with Tbsp. olive oil. Cover and simmer over medium heat for 45 minutes. Stir occasionally. If sauce thickens too much, add additional water.

Remove the carrot, garlic cloves and bay leaves. Add the Feta and using a handheld mixer or regular blender, process the sauce to smooth consistency.

- Cook 1 lb. pasta (*protein plus, gluten-free or wheat*). Drain and add to the sauce with 2-tbsp. olive oil. Toss well to combine
- Can be served topped with fresh arugula and cooked cubed or shredded chicken
- Roasted spaghetti squash is great alternative to regular pasta
- Fresh baby spinach can be substituted
- Sweet potato or Zucchini spirals can be substituted for grain pasta

Kale Torta!

Filling
1 garlic, minced
1 c chopped onion
4 oz. fresh spinach
1 beaten egg
Sundried tomatoes, optional

1 -recipe Focaccia Flatbread
8 oz. fresh kale
tsp. anchovy paste
½ c fresh parsley
½ c Feta cheese crumbles
Grated Romano to top

For the filling: Sauté the onions, garlic, anchovy paste in Tbsp. olive oil until soft and tender. Add the kale/spinach and stir continuously until wilted. Pour mixture into food processor, add the parsley, cheese and process until combined. Let cool.

Roll dough out on floured surface to fit the type of baking dish. I used an 8" fluted tart pan. Press dough into pan. Brush bottom and sides of dough w/oil and small amount of beaten egg. Add the remaining egg to the greens and stir. Fill the pan evenly and top with sundried tomatoes. Bake 30 minutes. Top with grated Romano cheese. Let cool before removing from pan.

> ➤ Purchased pie crust is an option but not healthy or hearty
> ➤ This can be made calzone style, but rolling dough larger, placing filling on one-side and folding remaining dough over, pinching, sealing, then baking. Be sure to put air holes in top prior to baking with this method

Orecchiette and Anchovies

8 oz. gluten-free Orecchiette pasta
1 garlic clove, minced
1 tomato, diced
Salt/pepper/Olive oil

3 anchovy fillets
handful fresh basil, chopped
1 c dark beer or white wine

Cook the pasta, drain and rinse. In a sauté pan, over medium-high heat, add 2-Tbsp. olive oil, minced garlic, tomato, anchovies. Cook until tender, stirring occasionally. Add the beer or white, salt/pepper and continue cooking 2-3 minutes. Add the cooked pasta, toss well to coat, add the basil.

Serve warm.

- Can be topped with cooked diced chicken or turkey
- Handful of fresh spinach can also be added
- Can be made spicy with hot pepper seeds
- Top with small amount grated parmesan cheese

Pistachio Crusted Chicken

This is a great gluten-free, high protein option!

2-chicken breast, no skin   1 c shelled pistachios
2 tbsp. corn meal   ¼ c Dijon or whole-grain mustard
2-Tbsp. raw honey

Seasonings: salt, pepper, ¼ tsp. dried thyme, tsp. dried oregano & parsley

Preheat oven to 400. In a food processor, finely grind the pistachios – be careful not to make butter ☺

In a bowl, add the chopped pistachios, cornmeal and seasonings, stir to combine. In a separate bowl, whisk together the Dijon and honey.

Brush 1-side of chicken with the mustard and honey. Dredge in the pistachio mixture; then do other side. Place on parchment or sil-pat lined baking sheet. Bake 35-40 minutes. Let cool before cutting.

Notes:

- If I had to do this over, I would have pounded the chicken out thin or purchased cutlets. It would have been easier to handle and quicker to cook
- These are delicious, sliced on the diagonal and served atop a bed of dark greens, lots of colorful veggies with light citrus vinaigrette.
- Gluten-Free flour can be used instead of corn meal

Quinoa Boats

1 recipe Quinoa Pesto   2-small zucchini

Halve lengthwise zucchini; using a small spoon, scrape out the flesh/seeds. Drizzle with olive oil, salt and pepper.

Fill with quinoa pesto. Can be served cold or at room temperature.

> ➢ To serve warm; Fill zucchini and bake at 350 for 20 minutes or to desired consistency.

Roasted Red Pepper Quinoa

1 c cooked/cooled white quinoa
¼ c minced onion
1" cube minced ginger root

1 ea. red, yellow & orange peppers
1 minced garlic clove
1-2 Tbsp. olive oil

Seasonings: salt, pepper, 1/8 tsp. dried thyme, tsp. dried oregano & basil, ¼ c minced parsley

Char the peppers until they are black on all sides and bottom. Place in a glass bowl, cover with plastic wrap and let cool. Remove the outside blackened skin and seeds. Place flesh in food processor. Process until well combined and texture is smooth. A small splash of water or broth may help.

Sauté the minced onion, ginger and garlic in of olive oil until translucent. Add the pureed peppers and seasonings. Stir until well combined and cook over low heat about 5-minutes to combine all flavors. Stir in the cooked quinoa and serve warm.

Notes:

- To make prep a little easier, I processed the onion, ginger and garlic in a food processor. This guarantees no large chunks
- The quinoa can be cooked in vegetable or chicken broth to additional flavor
- A gas grill or gas burners can be used to char the peppers. Use tongs to ensure safety
- I placed peppers on a baking sheet, with tin foil and used my broiler on high. I used tongs and continued to rotate the peppers until blackened on all sides

Spaghetti Squash

1 spaghetti squash, halved & seeded   Salt/Pepper
Tbsp. Olive oil

Preheat oven to 425. Season flesh with olive, salt and pepper. Place flesh side down, skin side up, on a silicone or parchment lined baking sheet. Roast 45 minutes or until tender. Remove; cool before using fork to scrape into spaghetti strings.

Serving options:

➤ Warm your favorite marinara sauce. Serve over warmed squash
➤ Halve, lengthwise and remove seeds from small zucchini. Season with salt, pepper and olive oil. Roast 425 for 15 minutes, until tender. Serve spaghetti squash in the zucchini boats, top with hot pepper seeds and grated parmesan cheese

Sweet Potato Risotto

3 sweet potatoes, peeled, cubed
1 yellow pepper, cored and cubed
½ onion, minced

½ c white wine
4 c vegetable or chicken broth
1 c Arborio rice

Seasonings: Salt, pepper, Dried parsley, ½ tsp. vanilla extract, 3 sprigs fresh mint chopped, ¼ c pecorino or parmesan cheese, pinch cinnamon, Olive oil, Tbsp. plain Greek yogurt

Preheat oven to 450. On baking sheet, lined with silicone or parchment, add sweet potato and yellow pepper. Drizzle with olive oil, salt, pepper and parsley. Roast for 20 minutes.

In a small saucepan, add broth and bring to simmer. Keep on low to maintain temp.

In large skillet, over medium-high heat, add tbsp. olive oil and onion. Stir occasionally until tender. Season with salt pepper and tsp. dried parsley. Add the risotto and stir; lightly toasting about 3-minutes. Add the white wine and stir. Once absorbed, begin adding the warm broth ½ c at a time, stirring frequently; continue adding liquid as each ½ c absorbs. Total rice cooking time is 20 minutes.

Add the roasted veggies, cheese, and remaining seasonings. Stir and serve immediately.

I have trained myself to eat lots of different foods over the years because I know my body needs the nutrients. Even if I don't like them, I've learned how, through alteration, experimentation and consistency, to get them into my body. Mushrooms are a great example. I don't like them… strongly do not like them. But, I found a way to incorporate them and not be able to taste them at all.

Turkey Sliders with Mushroom Kale Pesto

Makes: 8 mini-sliders, 4-larger patties

1 lb ground turkey
¼ c onion
Tbsp. Dijon

3 mushrooms *(any type, I used bella)*
2-Handful of greens *(kale, spinach)*
Tsp. each ground flax and chia seeds

Seasonings: salt, pepper, Tbsp. each of dried parsley, basil, oregano, tsp. cumin and coriander

In food processor, add the greens, onion and mushrooms until finely ground. Add to turkey with remaining seasonings. Mix by hand until thoroughly combined. Form sliders, patties or meatballs. Bake on 350 for 20-25 minutes or Sauté lightly in oil until done.

- ⑥ Sundried tomatoes make a great addition to this. *(3-4 added to processor)*.
- ⑥ To make spicy, add tsp. cayenne or a jalapeno to the food processor

This is another great way to use the Flatbread Focaccia Recipe; Or purchased whole wheat or gluten-free pizza crust can be substituted.

Tuscan White Bean Pizza

1 tomato, sliced
1-can drained and rinsed white beans
Tsp. each dried oregano and basil

Provolone cheese, shredded
Salt, Pepper
1-12" dough

Preheat oven to 425. Bake dough first; cool slightly, then top with white beans, slices of tomato, cheese, herbs and bake until warmed and melted. Cooked, cubed chicken can be added as well.

MINI-SWEET ENDINGS

Chocolate "Tricky" Brownies

Original recipe provided by www.sneakychef.com. *Altered by Theresa Hill*

3 Tbsp. butter
3 Tbsp. goat cheese
2 eggs
½ c sugar
¼ c + 2 Tbsp. gluten free flour
1-Tbsp. cocoa powder

¾ c dark chocolate chips
pinch salt
1 tsp. Vanilla
½ c *"Purple Puree" (recipe below)*
¼ c oats – finely ground
Tsp. of chia seeds

PURPLE PUREE

1 ½ c fresh kale; ½ c arugula; ¾ c fresh blueberries; tsp. orange juice & zest *(process until smooth consistency in food processor)*

Preheat oven to 350. In medium-sized bowl, melt butter, goat cheese and chocolate in microwave and let cool. In separate bowl, beat together eggs, sugar, vanilla, & **Purple Puree** until well incorporated. Add chocolate mixture and stir to combine.

In separate bowl, whisk together salt, cocoa & oats. Add to wet ingredients. Stir to combine.

I used a 10" x 7" baking dish; spray with non-stick, add batter and bake 350 for 30 minutes. Let cool before cutting.

There is no way I can leave out a Chocolate recipe! I love really dark chocolate. It's really the only sweet treat that I can have and in small amounts, it has great health benefits. Rich in antioxidants and minerals.

Chocolate Honey Pie

8 oz. dark chocolate chips (I use 80% or higher)   1 c toasted almonds
¼ c flour   ¼ c raw honey
¼ c hot water (in bowl)   4 eggs
½ c non-dairy butter (I use earth balance)   2 tsp. vanilla
½ tsp. cinnamon

Preheat oven to 350. In a food processor, add 4 oz. of the chips, nuts and flour. Remove to a bowl. In bowl of hot water, melt remaining chips and honey. Add to processor with the eggs, non-dairy butter, vanilla and cinnamon. Pulse to combine. Add chips/nut mixture and pulse again.

Pour into oiled/floured pie pan. Bake 35 minutes. Once cool, refrigerate for 2-hours to set.

➤ Gluten-free flour can be substituted for regular flour.
➤ Any nuts can be used (pistachios or walnuts would be great)
➤ A kick of spice makes this interesting; adding a ¼ tsp. cayenne is optional

Citrus Bundt Cake

6 oz. goat cheese
¼ c dairy-free butter (*earth balance*)
2 c sugar
1 c buttermilk
1 c Gluten-free flour blend
Tsp. baking powder

¼ c oil (*grapeseed, olive or canola*)
zest & juice of 1-orange, 1-lemon
4 eggs
tsp. vanilla
1 ½ c white flour
½ tsp. baking soda & salt

Topping: Fresh raspberries and melted white chocolate

Preheat oven to 350. In a bowl, add all dry ingredients and citrus zests, whisk to combine.

In another bowl, add the goat cheese, oil, dairy free butter, vanilla and sugar. Cream together with a mixer on medium-high for 2-3 minutes. Add the citrus juice, and mix until combined. With mixer running, add the eggs 1-at-1-time. Alternate the buttermilk and flour mixture in 3rds until combined. Scrap sides down and blend again. Be cautious not to overmix.

If using a Bundt pan, oil/flour the inside and add batter. Bake for 50 minutes or until golden brown and set.

If using 2- 9" round cake pans, use parchment on bottom. Add batter evenly to each pan. Bake for 30 min

I get asked all the time, "which protein bars do you recommend?" answer, "none". I am not an advocate for protein bars or powders so I created a version of my own.

Energy Bars

3.5 oz. bag of dried blueberries/cranberries
Tbsp. each of chia & ground flax seeds
1-egg
1/8 c dark brown sugar
½ c chopped nuts (*almond, walnuts, pistachios, any preference*)

¾ c quick oats
½ c almond or cashew butter
2 Tbsp. honey
¼ c golden raisins

Seasonings: pinch salt & nutmeg, ¼ tsp. dried ginger and cinnamon

Preheat oven to 350. In a small bowl, add dried fruit, raisins, oats, chia, flax, chopped nuts, seasonings and whisk to combine. In a larger bowl, beat with mixer the almond butter, egg, honey and dark brown sugar until creamy. Add the dry to the wet and beat just until combined.

Brush olive oil on bottom and sides of 8 ½ x 8 ½ glass dish. Using spatula, press the mixture evenly on bottom.

Bake 20 minutes. Cool entirely before cutting into bars. Store in airtight container in fridge. Keeps 7-days. Can be frozen for later use

Notes:

➢ Be sure the flax seeds are pre-ground. Never use whole flax seeds
➢ Melted dark chocolate can be drizzled over the top
➢ Pinch of cayenne pepper can be added to seasonings for a bit of a kick

Rosemary Olive Oil Cake

1 flour
2 tsp. baking powder
1 c sugar
2 tsps. Orange & lemon zests
¾ c Extra-virgin olive oil
2 Tbsps. Fresh minced rosemary

½ c cornmeal
½ tsp. salt
3 eggs
¼ c plain, fat-free yogurt
½ c chopped walnuts or almonds

NOTE: I used ½ c brown rice flour and ½ c Teft flour instead of white to increase the nutrients.

Preheat oven to 350. Spray pam on 1-Round 8" cake pan. Whisk together, flour, baking powder, and salt.

In separate bowl, beat sugar, eggs and zests until pale and doubled in volume (approx. 3 minutes). Add yogurt and gradually add oil while beating. Add the flour mixture in thirds. Stir in the chopped nuts.

Bake 35-45 minutes until golden brown and set in middle. Cool and dust top w/powdered sugar. This is a light, citrus inspired desired that pairs well with berries or orange segments.

Conclusion

We were not meant to do this life alone. God created us to need other people. He went to the cross for the purpose of creating a relationship opportunity with us and the Father. *Petite Plates* isn't just about simplifying, downsizing your meals, and eating plans. It's also about training—training our minds and bodies because they aren't ours – we were bought at a price and our bodies are God's vessels (**1 Cor. 9:27**). "What we feed grows, what we starve dies" (*Joyce Meyer*). What are we feeding not only our bodies, but our minds, eyes, ears? Are we starving our eyes and ears from negative things? What we put in our bodies through our mouths, affects our health in every way; simultaneously what we permit our eyes to see, ears to hear effects the way we act, speak as well as our daily choices. I would encourage each person who reads this book to surround themselves with positive influences that can not only inspire but also call you to a higher standard. Accept and invite challenge into your life. Change is in the struggle when approached with the right attitude. Suit up and go into battle with your health. Don't back off of when it gets hard, dig deep and keep on keeping on.

I honor these women; they are so important to me. They have helped, encouraged, and spoken truth to me and I'm grateful. Through my interactions with them, and countless others, I've learned the value of good quality relationships and the impact they can have on my life. **Galatians 6:2** *"Carry each other's burdens, and in this way you will fulfill the law of Christ."*

Praying that those who read this are encouraged, convicted and willing to make changes to improve their health.

Ezra 10:4 *"Rise up; this matter is in your hands. We will support you, so take courage and do it."*

EatWell my friends!
Theresa Hill, CDM, CFPP, Cookbook Author

About the Author

Theresa A. Hill is an accomplished writer, speaker, health advocate, and educator who lives and works in North Central West Virginia. Petite Plates is her second book, as she continues to create avenues of reaching people in the region and beyond with her ideas about health, wellness, and nutrition. In addition to her books, Theresa has spoken at many local charities and other events and has appeared on numerous local television spots promoting health and wellness. She has also had a number of articles written about her books and recipes in local newspapers and publications.

Theresa graduated with a degree in Dietary Management from Pierpont University in 2014, when she went back to school after raising her family. As a Certified Dietary Manager (CDM), she began a nutritional consulting business in 2015 called EatWell, LLC (www.eatwellLLC.wix.com/thill) . In her consulting role, she has worked with a variety of clients to help them meet their dietary, nutritional, or weight loss needs; including her husband Rick who was her very first client. By following Theresa's exercise advice and meal plan, Rick was able to lose 57 lbs. in 8 months, after struggling for nearly 20 years with his weight.

Theresa also works as a personal chef for certain clients creating weekly menus and preparing quality meals with high nutritional content for the entire family. She is most passionate about children and the poor eating habits that many of them have developed in today's culture. She creatively finds new ways to make traditional meals so that kids can learn that eating healthy can taste good too.

Theresa believes that God has given her gifts and abilities to be used in this place, at this time, for the people he places in her life. She serves with passion, and gives all the glory to God.

Printed in the United States
By Bookmasters